PHOTOGRAPHY BY N. JANE ISELEY

# BEAUFORT

HISTORIC BEAUFORT FOUNDATION, BEAUFORT, SOUTH CAROLINA

*In appreciation for her commitment to historic preservation*
*in Beaufort, South Carolina, this book is affectionately dedicated to*
*Helen Coggeshall Harvey*

PHOTOGRAPHY © 2003 / N. Jane Iseley
TEXT © 2003 / Historic Beaufort Foundation

ACKNOWLEDGEMENTS / This book would not have been possible
without the kindness and generosity of the many owners of the houses who
graciously allowed us to visit and photograph. Historic Beaufort Foundation and the photographer
are deeply grateful for their cooperation and hospitality.

ADDITIONAL THANKS / Maxine Fell Lutz, Jefferson Garland Mansell & Isabella Stuart Reeves

PHOTOGRAPHY COORDINATOR & STYLIST / Alice Turner Michalak
DESIGN / Palmetto Graphic Design Company
EDITOR / Sheryl Krieger Miller
PROOFREADER / Kathleen Zahnow Orfanedes

ISBN / 0-9657891-1-X
LIBRARY OF CONGRESS CONTROL NUMBER / 2002114080

HISTORIC BEAUFORT FOUNDATION / 713 Craven Street, Beaufort, SC 29902

PREPRESS / NEC, Nashville, Tennessee
PRINTING / Friesens, Altona, Manitoba, Canada

FOLLOWING SPREAD / Bay Street, Beaufort, South Carolina
*Reproduction of a copy by an unknown artist of a lost 1798 original by John Barnwell Campbell.*
*Courtesy of The Beaufort County Library, Beaufort, SC. Reproduction prints available exclusively at*
*The Beaufort County Public Library, 311 Scott Street, Beaufort, SC*

INTRODUCTION / *Primary sources used for the introduction include* A Guide to Historic Beaufort, *9th edition,*
*and* The Beaufort Preservation Manual *by John Milner & Associates, 1979.*

"In Beaufort one is conscious of the very antithesis of the modern
spirit of rush, and crowding, and haste . . . it is positively soothing to let one's thoughts
travel to and stay in such a place as Beaufort."

— *William Rotch Ware* | The Grandeur of the South

VISITORS ARE CAPTIVATED BY THE SMALL-
town charm, the natural beauty, and the magnificent architecture of Beaufort, South Carolina.
With gleaming white houses perched precariously close to the
water's edge and the soaring spires of churches rising majestically above the canopies of live oaks, Beaufort is a picturesque
city tucked away along the banks of the Beaufort River and the
intracoastal waterway. It has often been said that "one has to
be going to Beaufort; one never simply passes through it." This
relative isolation has played a large part in the preservation of
the town's historic architecture — a collection of hundreds of
residential and commercial buildings that reflect three centuries
of Beaufort's history since its founding in the early 1700s.

After 1520, when a Spanish explorer from Hispaniola
sailed into Port Royal Sound and named the area Santa
Elena, the Spanish, French, and English battled in their
efforts to colonize what they felt was a strategic location in
the New World. By the 1700s, English planters and traders
had established a firm foothold, and as early as 1706, they
may have constructed a block house near the river to protect
inland passage. In 1710, the Lords Proprietors, the counselors
and supporters of Charles II who had been granted the lands
known as Carolina, agreed that a seaport town should be
erected on the Sea Islands at the strategic point near the
confluence of two tidal streams. The new settlement was
named Beaufort Town in honor of one of the successor
Lords Proprietors, Henry Somerset, Duke of Beaufort.

Consisting originally of 397 lots, Beaufort's plan was
similar in concept to its sister city to the north, Charles Town
(Charleston). At Beaufort, the two areas of focus for the new
city were the front lots along the bay and four public lots
that formed a public square or civic center at the intersection
of Carteret and Craven streets. An act of the Provincial
Council required every person who took front lots to build

within two years, whereas owners of back lots were given an additional year. Unfortunately, the development of Beaufort was delayed by the Yemassee War in 1715 in which many of the Lowcountry Indian tribes rose in revolt. Led by the Yemassee tribe, the Indians attacked the young town of Beaufort, torturing and killing many of the settlers. After the rebellion was crushed and the Yemassee Indians took refuge in Spanish Florida, the surviving colonists returned and began rebuilding their burned-out homes.

In 1717, the first land grants were recorded, and early residential construction seems to have occurred at the four corners of New and Port Republic streets. While no early house within the city has survived as it was built, one house at this intersection provides a glimpse of the plan and form of Beaufort's early architecture. Reported to have been constructed as early as 1717, the Thomas Hepworth House is the earliest dwelling to survive. Although altered over time, it continues to be representative of Beaufort's colonial period.

Typically, these early Beaufort houses (1718–1750) were timber framed and built on raised foundations of tabby, an early form of concrete consisting of sand, oyster shells, and lime. The houses were either one-and-a-half-story or two-story structures that were one-room deep, consisting of an adjacent hall and parlor or a hall, parlor, and central passage. For the framing and finish work, builders used local materials such as heart pine and cypress found in nearby fresh-water swamps. Interior rooms were finished with plaster or paneling embellished with horizontal wainscoting. Glass panes and brick were scarce commodities in colonial Beaufort. Indeed, as late as March 1733, Thomas Causton, a colonist on his way to Georgia, passed through Beaufort and noted, "The houses there are all of timber and very few have glass windows or brick chimneys."

The builders and occupants of Beaufort's earliest houses included Barbadian planters, French Huguenots, English indentured servants, tradesmen, and religious dissenters, all who arrived on the banks of the Beaufort River seeking their fortunes. During the colonial period, naval stores and provision crops were the economic mainstay of the Beaufort area, but the largest fortunes were made in trade and the cultivation of indigo, from which blue dye was derived.

Shipbuilding was also an important industry, centered primarily along Bay Street and on Black's Point on the eastern edge of town. There were three dry-goods stores on Bay Street, and the adjacent wharfs served ships that connected Beaufort with Charleston, Savannah, and the larger cities of the coastal colonies. Additionally, Beaufort became an important port of entry for the expanded trade in African slaves. The increased population and the expansion of indigo production accelerated the demand for slave labor. By the eve of the Revolution, an unidentified English traveler was able to report that Beaufort was "a well peopled good-looking town, better than half the size of Charleston."

Although there was a brief period of economic depression following the Revolution, prosperity returned to Beaufort in the 1790s as technological innovations dramatically changed local agricultural practices. With the declining interest in indigo, planters began experimenting with alternative cash crops. For a short time, after the invention of the husking mill, a tidal rice culture flourished. Nevertheless, it was the cultivation of a variety of long-staple cotton and the invention of the cotton gin that gave rise to the great fortunes of Beaufort-area planters. This particular strain of cotton was easily separated from its seeds by the large slave labor force that was to become an integral part of the local economy. Sea Island cotton quickly became recognized as the finest and most expensive product in America. The planter elite, riding the wave of prosperity, began constructing villas along the high bluffs of the Beaufort River. These planters viewed Beaufort as a summer resort, an ideal retreat from the dangers of fever and the swarms of insects found at their island plantations.

PHOTOGRAPHY BY ALICE TURNER MICHALAK

constructed scores of similar T-shaped houses throughout the town. These design elements became so commonplace in local residential architecture that houses incorporating these characteristics are often referred to as being in the "Beaufort style."

Beaufort planters and builders, with their social and economic ties to Charleston, naturally turned to their sister city for architectural inspiration. A series of fine Federal-era Beaufort residences resemble the English Palladian mansions that line Charleston streets. Built between 1780 and 1805, these Beaufort houses featured tabby walls or foundations, hipped roofs, and central halls that widened in the rear to accommodate a single flight of stairs rising to a landing, dividing into two flights, and returning to the second story along opposite sides of the hall. Venetian windows lit the landings, and the interiors were finished with elegant carved wood and cast plaster that reflected the influence of Robert Adam, the popular late-18th-century English architect. In contrast to earlier Beaufort houses, these Adam-Palladian dwellings exhibited a major new architectural device, a projecting pedimented portico supported by slender Tuscan columns.

These prominent porches are evident in the earliest known image of Beaufort: John Campbell's 1798 painting that captures the parade of mansions stretching along the banks of the Beaufort River. Elegant Federal-style houses stand in stark contrast to the more utilitarian stores and warehouses along the waterfront. Through the 1830s, the Federal style dominated Beaufort architecture. Vernacular house forms

While Beaufort, Charleston, and Savannah developed simultaneously, each created their own distinctive architecture. In Savannah and Charleston, the architecture was decidedly urban in character, reflecting their status as important trading centers and port cities. Their townhouses were designed to conform to and make the most of constricted city lots. Beaufort's character and architecture were quite different. Although recognized as a port and as a resort, Beaufort remained small and remote. Beaufort's houses, free-standing and located on spacious lots, resemble the architecture of the Southern plantation — large-scale houses seemingly more appropriate for vast estates than narrow village streets.

Beaufort architecture also reflects accommodations that were necessary to survive in the often stifling heat of Lowcountry summers. Houses were constructed on raised basements with southern orientations in an attempt to capture the slightest breeze off the Beaufort River. One-story and double-tiered porches provided shade and became inviting outdoor living spaces. The common T-shaped floor plan, where rear chambers on either side of the hallway project beyond the width of the façade, allowed for maximum cross-ventilation. This floor plan was so conducive to the local climate that Beaufort's unidentified builders and master craftsmen

were embellished with fan-lights, geometric gouge work, and Venetian windows — decorative elements drawn from the Federal vocabulary. The conservative planters and merchants of Beaufort contin-ued to build their Adam Palladian mansions until the 1840s, when they embraced

PHOTOGRAPHY BY ALICE TURNER MICHALAK

Greek Revival architecture, a national style that had begun sweeping across America in the 1820s.

Between 1852 and 1860, Beaufort witnessed the greatest construction activity of the 19th century, as scores of new houses, a church, and a college building were constructed in the Greek style. The owners of older homes, eager to show that they, too, were cognizant of the prevailing fashionable trends in domestic architecture, launched extensive remodeling programs. The delicate porches of the Federal era gave way to monumental verandas, and simple flat moldings and wide trim replaced the old-fashioned intricately carved wood and cast-plaster interior details. Glass was now plentiful, and tall first-floor windows and doors with rectangular transoms and sidelights replaced the small multi-pane sash windows, the arched fanlights, and the Venetian windows. In the 1850s, six impressive Greek Revival mansions were built at the eastern end of Bay Street and on Black's Point.

While Beaufort planters may have been reluctant to abandon the Federal style, by the late 1850s, they were eagerly experi-menting not only with Greek Revival but with Italianate and Gothic architecture, as well. With wide-overhanging eaves, tall windows, cupolas, and extensive porches, Italianate archi-tecture was well-suited for the Southern climate. Beaufort

planter Edgar Fripp found an ideal plan for an Italian villa in Design I of Samuel Sloan's *The Model Architect*, an important pattern book published by the prominent Philadelphia architect in 1852. Undoubtedly, Beaufort's ama-teur builders and craftsmen relied heavily on pattern books to provide plans, perspectives, and elevations in a variety of architectural styles. In 1852, as Beaufort became a center of secessionist fever and local citizens sensed that an increase in local military protection was needed, John Gibbes Barnwell, commander of the Beaufort Volunteer Artillery, refurbished the old 1798 Arsenal in the Gothic Revival style. With a crenellated parapet, pointed arched windows, and slender buttresses, the fortress-like appearance of the Arsenal provided an appropriate symbol of civil authority. Most Beaufortonians, however, simply selected decorative elements and applied them to their more classically inspired dwellings. Brackets, octagonal columns, and pierced woodwork balustrades were picturesque details found on a number of Beaufort's last great antebellum mansions.

By 1860, Beaufort was described as the "wealthiest, most aristocratic, and most cultivated town of its size in the country." Sir Charles Lyell, an English geologist, described Beaufort as "a picturesque … assemblage of villas, the summer residences of numerous planters. … Each villa is shaded by a verandah, surrounded by beautiful live oaks and orange trees laden with fruit." Planters enjoyed the pursuits of the English gentry, including horse racing, hunting, and fishing. A favorite male pastime was assembling to "eat, drink, and talk politics and planting." As 1860 drew to a close, their political discussions focused on secession. On December 20, 1860, the secessionist convention declared South Carolina's independence from the Union. In little less than a year, a Federal fleet attacked and took Forts Walker and Beauregard at the entrance to the Port Royal harbor. Beaufort planters and their families fled, abandoning their plantations and townhouses in what one war correspondent called "The Grand Skedaddle." Occupying Federal troops used Beaufort's mansions and churches as hospitals, administrative offices, and staff quarters. Due to its early occupation by Federal forces, Beaufort escaped the destruction wrought on many Southern cities, although most residents never returned, particularly after losing their property at the Federal Government's direct tax sale of 1863.

The Civil War brought sweeping social and political changes to Beaufort. The slave labor system was eradicated, and the cotton-based economy was ruined. New construction was limited to church buildings that served independent African-American congregations. After the war, freedmen poured into Beaufort to take advantage of educational opportunities and the access to property. Many African-Americans settled in the northwest section of town, building or renovating small cottages and creating a distinctive community.

In the 1870s, Beaufort's economy recovered with the development of phosphate mining and the revival on a limited scale of Sea Island cotton production. Beaufort also became a winter resort for Northerners. Beaufort's streetscapes began

*Beaufort also became a winter resort . . . streetscapes began to change as modestly scaled and moderately priced Victorian houses rose on the lots adjacent to antebellum mansions. These houses reflected not only a change in architectural taste but in the composition of the town's population.*

to change, as modestly scaled and moderately priced Victorian houses rose on the lots adjacent to antebellum mansions. These houses reflected not only a change in architectural taste but in the composition of the town's population. Northern and immigrant merchants constructed two-story frame houses loosely based on Queen Anne and Stick styles and constructed with sawn timber instead of hand-hewn posts. Bay windows and turrets, as well as commercially milled spindle work, turned posts, and gingerbread adorned the facades of new houses and quickly appeared on older updated dwellings.

Beaufort's economic future looked bright, especially after the U.S. government established the U.S. Marine Corps Post on Parris Island in 1891. Unfortunately, in 1893, a major hurricane ripped through the town, coming ashore at high tide and completely covering the Sea Islands. Scores of buildings were damaged, thousands were drowned, and the phosphate industry was destroyed. Beaufort had barely recovered when disaster struck again in 1907. A fire at a local cotton warehouse swept through downtown, jumping about as it pushed northward along the western edge of Black's Point, consuming stores, warehouses, cotton gins, and a number of Federal-era mansions. After each disaster, Beaufortonians repaired and rebuilt their dwellings along the lines of current architectural fashions, employing modern building techniques. Slowly, the once distinctive Beaufort style began to wane as local residential construction mirrored architectural styles found throughout the country. The cottages and bungalows of the

early 20th century made no reference to the region's architectural past. Instead, they represented Beaufort's embracement of mainstream American architecture.

After the installation of large military bases in 1941, Beaufort experienced a sudden population explosion as well as a local housing shortage. Along Bay Street and throughout the older neighborhoods, antebellum mansions and Victorian houses were subdivided into apartment buildings and tenements. The post-war housing boom gave rise to large-scale construction south and west of the original town boundaries. As families began to move into new residential areas, the old neighborhoods began to decline.

By 1942, the John Mark Verdier House, commonly known as the Lafayette Building and one of Beaufort's finest Federal-era houses, had deteriorated and was condemned. Concerned with losing one of its principal landmarks, the local community rallied, and in 1945 they established the "Committee to Save the Lafayette Building."

After purchasing the Bay Street property, the committee spent the next 20 years completing a major renovation. By the mid-1960s, the leaders of this committee recognized the need for an organization to take on the larger responsibility for preserving Beaufort's historic architecture. In 1965, they formed the Historic Beaufort Foundation.

Since its creation, the Foundation has played a major leadership role in preserving the cultural resources and historic landmarks of Beaufort County. After initiating the first architectural survey of the city in 1968, the Foundation created

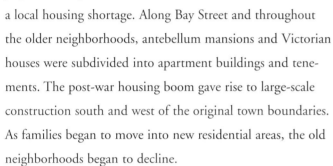

Beaufort's first historic district. In 1975, the district was designated a National Historic Landmark, one of only a handful of districts in South Carolina to be so recognized. The Foundation's Revolving Fund has been used to purchase and restore a number of buildings, from large, imposing mansions on Bay Street to the small vernacular cottages in the western edge of the district. In 2001, with generous financial assistance from city and county governments, the Foundation assumed the operation of the Beaufort Museum and began a major renovation of the former Arsenal, creating an interpretive center of local history for residents and an ever-increasing number of tourists.

An early 20th-century visitor once wrote, "After a week in Beaufort I was loth to leave … but the entering wedge of modern and so-called advanced civilization is forcing its way in; but it will take a long time to modernize sleepy old Beaufort." The picturesque town resting atop the bluffs of the river has been discovered, however, and each year Beaufort welcomes tens of thousands of visitors who come to experience the charm of the South Carolina Lowcountry.

As the city and the surrounding region experience unprecedented growth, Beaufort is faced with its most serious challenge to date — the difficult task of protecting its fragile historic architecture and maintaining the wonderful quality of life it offers its residents. Nevertheless, Beaufort's collection of historic architecture reveals that it is an extraordinary place, a town that according to one writer continues to be "a monument to endurance."   —*Jefferson Garland Mansell*

# The John Mark Verdier House

*The stair hall is separated from the entrance hall by an archway, highlighted by engaged Corinthian columns (above). The reception room, or ballroom, is the most elaborately detailed space in the house (right). Cast-plaster relief panels and an ellipse framed by quadrant starburst motifs adorn the reception room's mantel (following spread).*

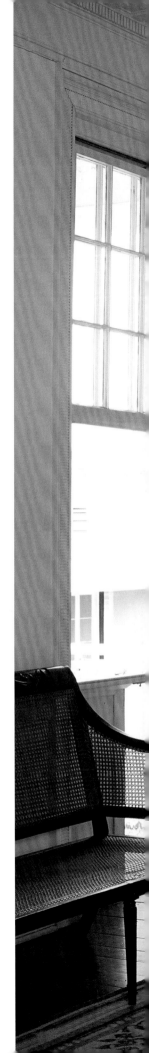

LIKE OTHER 18TH-CENTURY MERCHANTS and planters, John Mark Verdier made and lost his fortune a number of times in the rather unstable post-Revolutionary economic climate. Rising to great stature and wealth before the Revolution, Verdier's fortune was swept away as indigo markets disappeared with the war. After a short stay in a Charleston debtor's prison, Verdier returned to Beaufort and rode the next wave of prosperity — Sea Island cotton.

After re-establishing his mercantile interests and acquiring extensive plantation holdings, Verdier began construction on a townhouse befitting his position as a wealthy Sea Island planter. Located in the commercial heart of Beaufort, the Verdier House is a reminder that downtown Bay Street was once a thoroughfare lined with both fine residences and commercial buildings. Eighteenth-century merchants, like Verdier, often lived above, next door, or within close proximity to their businesses.

The name of the master builder or carpenter of Verdier's Federal-style home is unknown. The house is a close relation to Tabby Manse and the Elizabeth Barnwell Gough house, featuring a floor plan where the central hall widens in the rear to accommodate an imposing staircase.

*The focal point of the parlor is the
Fairfield County, S.C., secretary desk* (left).
*The dining room can be seen through the
parlor door* (above, left).
*The dining room contains a pair of mahogany
veneered English cutlery urns
c.1820. John Mark Verdier's initials
are found on the English sterling-silver tea
and coffee pots* (above, right).

Because of the relatively small commercial lot, Verdier could not use the common T-shaped plan that would have allowed the southern breeze to flow through the extended rear rooms. The result is a square, symmetrical house with a Palladian-inspired portico. The severe façade gives little hint of the elegant interior: richly detailed cypress paneling, cast-plaster mantels, and elaborate Corinthian pilasters supporting a molded semi-elliptical archway.

According to anecdotes, Gen. Lafayette addressed the citizens of Beaufort from Verdier's front portico in 1825. The family retained ownership into the 20th century although the house was no longer used as a single-family residence. Apartments and businesses gradually took over its interiors. By the 1940s, the "Lafayette Building," as the house had become known, had deteriorated and was condemned.

Slated for demolition to make way for a gas station, the house became the focal point for the town's first organized preservation effort. The Committee to Save the Lafayette Building purchased the property in 1946, renovating it for use as rental space. In 1967, the committee gave the property to its successor organization, the Historic Beaufort Foundation, which restored the property in 1976. The Verdier House, the Foundation's flagship property, serves as Beaufort's only historic house museum.

# The Robert Means House

*The restoration revealed elegantly decorated pine paneling* (above).
*The drawing room showcases a fine Adam-style mantel* (right).
***B**ottles and pottery shards excavated from a former privy provide insight into the lifestyles of previous owners of the house* (following spread).

---

**R**IDING THE WAVE OF PROSPERITY FOLLOWING the American Revolution, wealthy Beaufort planters built a series of townhouses along the west end of Bay Street, a neighborhood commonly referred to as The Bluff. With an ever-present breeze coming up the Beaufort River and close proximity to churches, the courthouse, and the commercial district, The Bluff was a prime residential location.

Around 1800, Robert Means constructed his two-story house and joined the Elliotts, Barnwells, and Fullers along what was becoming Beaufort's most fashionable street.

Like other houses of the time, Means' house was embellished with details drawn from the Federal style, such as the fanlight over the entrance and the Venetian window illuminating the staircase landing. The double-tiered porches with full-height Doric columns are an early 20th-century affectation, replacing the modest, original one-story porch. The home housed Union troops during the Civil War and was later home to Maj. Edward Denby, Secretary of the Navy under President Warren G. Harding and a participant in the Teapot Dome scandal of 1923.

Means' dwelling was subsequently converted into an apartment house, but a two-year restoration begun in 1995 returned the house to a private residence.

# The George Mosse Stoney House

**A** *local master craftsman created the mantel in the 2001 restoration* (above).
**Z***uber paper, "Hindustan," re-created with blocks used in the 1805 original, provides a colorful background in the dining room* (right).

JOHN CAMPBELL'S PAINTING OF BEAUFORT in 1798 shows the early Federal-style house that Dr. George Mosse Stoney remodeled in the Greek Revival style around 1840.

Stoney capitalized on his sweeping view of the Beaufort River and Lady's Island by adding the wide double piazzas supported by rows of fluted Doric columns. A pediment from the earlier house was retained and, along with the main cornice, embellished with wide bands of simple dentil molding. Stoney added rear rooms to the structure, which was originally one room deep, creating a classic T-shaped Beaufort house. Earlier Federal moldings were swept away and replaced with woodwork in the contemporary Greek fashion.

In 1866, Austrian jeweler Moritz Pollitzer, one of a number of European immigrants who arrived in post-Civil War Beaufort, purchased the home. Prominent in Beaufort politics and cultural life, the Pollitzers owned the property for five generations.

In the 1980s, the home was converted to condominiums, but in 2001, talented craftsmen and a sensitive homeowner undertook a major restoration that returned the house to a single-family dwelling. Once again, from its elegant interiors, visitors could gaze across the balustraded verandas and the brick-lined terraces and take in the glistening waters of the Beaufort River.

**A**n Oriental screen provides a backdrop for a comfortable mix of English and American
furniture and family mementos (left).
**A** *An inviting chaise lounge is a comfortable addition to the dressing room* (above).

# Orange Grove Plantation

PHOTOGRAPHY BY ALICE TURNER MICHALAK

*Orange Grove is situated on a unique finger of land along Capers Creek on one side and a series of ponds on the other* (above). *The garden is planted with tropical evergreens, including wild irises, windmill palms, nandinas, fatsia, holly ferns, and dwarf gardenias* (right).

SECLUDED ALONG CAPERS CREEK ON ST. Helena Island, Orange Grove was established by Peter Perry in the mid-1750s as a successful indigo plantation. A low tabby wall that surrounds the graves of Perry and Fripp family members remains as a reminder of a world that ended when Union troops occupied the area after the Battle of Port Royal Island in 1861.

The property declined in the years following Reconstruction. In 1928, Massachusetts Congressman Henry L. Bowles purchased it as a hunting retreat. He replaced the deteriorated plantation house with a gracious two-story raised cottage in the Cape Cod style. The property changed ownership twice afterward.

In 1964, the present owners acquired Orange Grove and have devoted their lives to careful enhancements to the house and grounds. The rear side of the house was opened with large sections of glass to provide panoramic views of the surrounding tidal creek and expansive marsh. Fresh-water ponds were developed on the east, providing an active habitat for bird life.

In 1972, the owners replaced the small east wing with additional living space and built a walled garden designed by the late Robert E. Marvin. Marvin was again called upon in 1999 to redesign the garden to include a sun pocket that works as an outdoor room, a multilevel water feature that attracts birds, and an arbor-covered deck for family dining.

# The William J. Whipper House

*An 1830 D.F. Blair muzzleloader*
*rests below the den mantel (above).*
*An inviting mixture of Queen Anne*
*and Windsor chairs are found in*
*the dining room. A collection of*
*20th-century advertising signs in*
*the kitchen is visible through*
*the open door (right).*

THE CHARM OF BEAUFORT'S HISTORIC district is the variety of its architecture, ranging from grand and imposing masonry mansions occupying full city blocks to small, frame cottages tucked away on narrow tree-lined streets.

Constructed between 1820 and 1840, this dwelling was owned by William J. Whipper, an African-American who became one of Beaufort's most powerful post-Civil War political figures.

The house was restored in the early 1970s. Presently, this one-and-a-half-story cottage provides a modest backdrop for an important collection of antiques and fine art.

Included in the collection are a number of 19th- and 20th-century landscape paintings and ikebana baskets.

The cannonball andirons in the den originally graced a fireplace at The Castle, the nearby Joseph Johnson House.

Seen in the above photograph of the den: The child's wing chair is from the 1790s; an assembly of English, American, and Australian croquet mallets is shown in the foreground.

An ivory chess set, c. 1840, and two Japanese burial figures rest on the mantel of the dining room (right).

# The Bold-Webb House

*The kitchen walls display Southern and Italian cooking utensils* (above).
*A Carolina Parrot from the American Bien edition of John Audubon's work is above the mantel* (right).
*The library paneling was made from lumber rescued from a house in Barnwell, S.C.* (following spread).

In 1809, Black's Point was incorporated into Beaufort. At that time, the eastern section of town was a mixture of industrial and residential development but still retained a decidedly rural atmosphere. A functioning tidal basin provided direct access to the surrounding Beaufort River. Originally much larger and extending east and west along King Street, the tidal basin provided an ideal location for a mill and shipbuilding activities.

In the late 18th century, William Bold's father constructed a dwelling that looked out over the tidal basin. The structure was one-room deep with a sleeping loft and had the appearance of a rural farmhouse. After inheriting the property in 1804, Bold may have enlarged the home for his ever-growing family.

Over the years, successive owners added necessary rooms, and renovations were made after the hurricane of 1893. The residence is similar to other Beaufort-area houses with its double porches supported by simple tapered posts and rear one-story rooms projecting past the façade to allow for cross-ventilation. In the late 20th century, the owner erected a replica of a historic house in Warrenton, Ga., to serve as a library and guesthouse. Located on the southern edge of the property, the new cottage is a faithful reproduction of the Federal-style dwelling.

# The Rev. Thomas E. Ledbetter House

*From his upstairs windows and the cool shade of his porch, Thomas Ledbetter enjoyed magnificent views of the Beaufort River to the north and the lush, park-like setting of his gardens to the south (above). The parlor windows and interior woodwork are part of repairs made to the house following the hurricane of 1893. Audubon drawings and 19th-century waterfowl prints adorn the walls of the parlor and hallway (right).*

and desolation."

A METHODIST MISSIONARY INTENT ON evangelizing Sea Island slaves, Thomas Ledbetter acquired the property in 1840 and immediately began construction on his Beaufort-style house. During a renovation in the late 1970s, workmen uncovered an inscription on a wall lath that read, "T.E. Ledbetter & Martin Eaddy missionaries at Beaufort and neighboring islands 1840 February."

Major changes to the house, including the addition of the second-floor piazza, occurred following the devastating hurricane of 1893. Capt. Neils Christensen, then owner of the property and superintendent of Beaufort's National Cemetery, described the devastation wrought by the massive storm in a letter to his wife:

"There is not a vestige left of the stable, carriage-house, etc. except part of the brick foundation. ... The brick seawall I built years ago was leveled, and the soil all the distance to the house was licked and scooped away by the waves — everything looks destruction

# The James Robert Verdier House / Marshlands

*The dining room contains 18th-century Maryland furniture, including the signed table and sideboard from Queen Anne's County and chairs made for General John Eager Howard (above). The central hallway with its matching fanlights is furnished with 18th-century American and English pieces, including two Virginia-made chairs (right).*

MARSHLANDS IS A HOUSE BEST VIEWED from the water. The white-frame dwelling with its red roof seems to float serenely above Beaufort's river marsh. In an attempt to determine the origins of Beaufort's early domestic buildings, architectural historians have labeled Marshlands as Barbadian or West Indian. Regardless of its architectural roots, Marshlands is a pure expression of the Beaufort style, a vernacular house form elegantly attired in Federal dress.

Painted the palest pink, the lower-level arcade supports a wraparound porch that commands a splendid view of the river and Lady's Island. Simple tapered porch columns stand in contrast to the exquisite fanlights, tripartite windows, and delicate moldings. The interior is rich in Federal detailing, with Adam-influenced mantels, reeded woodwork, interior fanlights, and a graceful spiraling staircase illuminated by a Palladian window.

Completed in 1814 by James Robert Verdier, Marshlands is listed as a National Historic Landmark. Architecturally significant, the house is also important as the home of Dr. Verdier, a physician who developed a successful treatment for yellow fever.

*The library paneling and the 18th-century French tiles were added
in the mid-20th century. Maps, prints and family photographs
adorn the paneled walls of the library* (left).
*The mahogany secretary is 18th-century English Chippendale.
In the drawing room, the 19th-century Louis XV style chair
retains its original needlepoint upholstery* (above).

# Wimbee Creek Farm

*Charleston silhouettist Carew Rice
designed the wrought-iron sign
for Myrtle Grove, a family plantation.
An 1826 French tin Alfa Romeo model
reveals a collector's interest in vintage
automobiles* (above).
*The den provides an ideal setting for
observing Lowcountry wildlife
in the surrounding marsh* (right).

Nestled between the marsh of
Wimbee Creek and three majestic live oaks,
this farmhouse was originally four separate
structures, all of which were rescued and
restored to create a charming modern home
from vintage Lowcountry buildings.

The plan is reminiscent of 18th-century
models with a central structure connected to
outlying pavilions by hallways. The ensemble
is tied together by a series of inviting porches
that offer views of the surrounding marshes
and farmland.

The owners purchased the property in
1982, and construction began as they
acquired a small collection of abandoned
and deteriorated historic structures.

A former detached kitchen and a small
house, both 19th-century buildings, were
relocated to the property from nearby
communities and attached to the early
20th-century house.

Wimbee Creek Farm's unique restoration
project took four years to complete. The result is a sprawling, modern country house that
appears to have evolved over centuries, as if it was added onto by subsequent generations
of an original builder.

**A** *1936 Ford Phaeton is parked in front of Wimbee Creek Farm — a charming home
created from four historic structures nestled under live oak trees* (previous spread).
**I**n *order to create library space, a small hallway was created between two guest rooms.
Fashioned out of heart pine and lit by high windows above the shelves, the reading room
makes for a cozy, yet practical space. A painting by Emmett Owen hangs on the far wall* (left).
**O**riginally *a barn, the dining room contains an eclectic mix of antiques,
including 18th-century Windsor chairs and a South Carolina china cabinet* (above).

# The John Lambeth House

*The compatibility of the late-20th-century addition to the original house is evident, as seen from the garden designed by Miss Clermont Lee, a prominent Savannah landscape architect (above).*
*Toni Cordero's art glass chandelier in the dining room is titled "Iside." Beaufort artist Lana Hefner painted "Coastal Storm" (right).*

For centuries, Beaufort home owners have been renovating and remodeling houses, making historic structures comfortable for contemporary living.

In the late 1980s, architect James Thomas designed a complementary addition to the east elevation of the Lambeth House, including a soaring glass-front kitchen and an east-facing porch that captures a stunning view of the Beaufort River.

The restoration of the original 1820 house revealed that an original Federal-style portico had been swept away and replaced by inviting double-tiered porches sometime in the mid-19th century.

The interior, however, retains its heart-pine floor, cypress paneling, and a pegged-cypress staircase.

*The living room features a dynamic blend of traditional and contemporary pieces. The Beaufort River can be seen in the distance* (left). *The extensive use of glass in the contemporary kitchen provides a light-filled work space* (above).

# The Berners Barnwell Sams House

*The transom and sidelights of the door frame a view of the Front Green. Slated for development in the early part of the 20th century, the Front Green was saved by Elizabeth Waterhouse, who purchased the Sams house in 1895 (above). The first floor of the portico provides elegant and inviting seating (right).*

IN THE DECADE BEFORE THE CIVIL WAR, the production of cotton gave rise to some of Beaufort's greatest fortunes and grandest mansions. In 1852, Dr. Berners Barnwell Sams, a local planter and part owner of Datha (Dataw) Island, began construction of his imposing Greek Revival townhouse.

The resulting mansion incorporates the locally popular T-shaped floor plan, a massive Greek Revival portico, and fanciful pierced woodwork balustrades and parapet.

B.B. Sams' house reflects the conservative nature of most Southern planters in the mid-19th century who were reluctant to abandon Greek Revival architecture altogether, yet wanted to include some elements of the more fashionable picturesque styles sweeping America.

While four monumental Doric columns rise to a heavy denticulated cornice, the pierced woodwork balustrade and parapet add a delicate and romantic tone to the heavy, classical façade. Unfortunately, B.B. Sams never enjoyed his creation. He died of pneumonia shortly before the home's completion in 1855.

At the rear of the property, a one-story brick and tabby dependency is believed to have housed a blacksmith shop, cook house, laundry, and slave quarters. It is one of the few surviving dependencies in Beaufort. The grounds include late-19th-century gardens and the remains of a tabby wall.

# The Prioleau House / Mooreland

*F*lanking pergolas in the magnificent
formal gardens mirror the classical lines
of the Colonial Revival home. (above).
*T*he glistening waters of the Beaufort River
are visible from the dining room (right).

THIS HOUSE RESTS ON THE TABBY FOUN-
DATION of an 18<sup>th</sup> century home depicted in
one of the earliest known paintings of
Beaufort. Built just before the 20<sup>th</sup> century
by Dr. A. P. Prioleau, the house is faithful to
the Beaufort-style design of its predecessor
with south facing double porches, a central
hall, and a T-shaped floor plan, leading many
to believe that the house is much older than it
is. The interior contains some of Beaufort's
best Colonial Revival interiors with wide
moldings and highly decorative mantles. The
home also incorporates a favorite regional
architectural device, large windows rest on jib
doors, which when open, allow easy access to
the porches and a sweeping vista of Beaufort
River.

During World War II, the house was divided into apartments. The Moore family, for
whom the structure is now named, subsequently restored the dwelling. After a succes-
sion of owners, the house underwent an
extensive renovation in 2002.

# Tidalholm

In an attempt to escape the heat and mosquitoes that made life on his St. Helena Island plantation intolerable, Edgar Fripp decided to build a summer home in Beaufort. The result was the town's best example of Italianate architecture.

With designs that incorporated wide overhanging eaves, large windows, and extensive porches, Italianate architecture was highly favored by Southern planters and their builders. Fripp's inspiration came from Design I of the popular pattern book, *The Model Architect*, first published by Philadelphia architect Samuel Sloan in 1852.

Sloan's published design included a small entrance porch, which would have offered little shade in the blistering summer heat of the Lowcountry. Either Fripp or Sloan revised the plan, providing for a deep one-story porch wrapping around three sides of the dwelling.

Originally, Tidalholm featured twin front-facing gables and a soaring central tower. Unfortunately, the distinctive tower and gables were damaged in the hurricane of 1893 and subsequently removed. The house was then modified by the addition of a spacious second-story porch under a simple gable roof.

# The Elizabeth Hext House / Riverview

RIVERVIEW IS ONE OF BEAUFORT'S OLDEST HOUSES. CONSTRUCTED BETWEEN 1765 AND 1780, IT was the home of planter William Sams and his wife, Elizabeth Hext of Datha (Dataw) Island. The house incorporates elements common in Lowcountry architecture, such as a raised basement and a south-facing symmetrical façade with double porches.

Illustrating early construction methods, the exterior walls support the main weight of the house. In an often oppressive climate, this construction technique allowed the interior walls to be relatively thin — in some cases, the thickness of a single piece of wood.

There's no doubt that the house provided a cool and welcomed retreat for William Sams' large family of 16 who moved to Beaufort to escape the unhealthy summer island climate.

# Pinckney Street Cottage

**A** *light-filled artist's studio provides the cottage with a stunning view of the Beaufort River* (above). **T***he main house, potting shed and mature garden, shown here in spring, appear to have existed since the early 20th century.*

**S**ET AMIDST SOME OF THE MOST IMPOSING mansions in Beaufort's historic district, this 20th-century ranch house was creatively renovated in 1991 to complement the architecture of the neighborhood and to take advantage of a spectacular view of the Beaufort River.

Using the best elements of Lowcountry architecture, the dwelling takes its cue from the numerous river cottages that once lined the marshes of Beaufort's streams and estuaries.

With extensive porches, banks of large windows, and the ubiquitous metal roof, the designer provided a comfortable and spacious modern home while maintaining the appearance of a modest cottage.

# The Joseph Hazel House

THE JOSEPH HAZEL HOUSE IS ADJACENT TO THE TIDAL BASIN, THE REMNANT OF A LARGER BODY OF water that originally wrapped around two sides of the small lot. Because of the constricted building area, Hazel positioned the double-tiered portico of his house directly on the street, allowing space at the rear of the house for the necessary outbuildings.

The interior of the house reflects the changing tastes of Beaufortonians in the 1840s. Decoration in some rooms follows Federal designs; in others, particularly the east parlor, the moldings are executed in the emerging Greek Revival style.

After the Battle of Port Royal Island, the house served as a Union hospital, quartering African-American soldiers from the 54th Massachusetts Regiment. The property remained in the Hazel family until 1936 and subsequently was used as an apartment house.

A 1980s renovation included reconstructing the original Federal-style portico.

# Tombee Plantation

**S**CORES OF PLANTATION HOUSES ONCE DOTTED ST. HELENA ISLAND. USUALLY OCCUPIED BY BEAUFORT planters only during the winter months, these homes were less elaborate than their Beaufort counterparts. In 1790, Thomas B. Chaplin constructed a two-story house ideally suited for the island climate, utilizing a common T-shaped plan. The house contains a central hall and flanking rooms with windows on three sides, allowing for maximum cross-ventilation. An additional room is located on both floors at the rear of the central hall. This particular plan was common not only on the islands but in the city of Beaufort as well.

The oldest surviving plantation house on St. Helena, Tombee is best known for the diary kept by the builder's grandson, also named Thomas B. Chaplin. In 1845, Chaplin, the master of Tombee, began to chronicle his daily activities, a practice he continued off and on for the next forty years. The published diary and an accompanying biography provide extraordinary insight into mid-19th-century plantation life on St. Helena Island.

The plantation was confiscated by Union troops and included in what became known as the Port Royal experiment, a Federal program that intended to construct a town for freedmen. The Port Royal Experiment was never completely realized.

# The Frederick Fraser House

**A** collection of first-edition Audubon prints of Beaufort-area birds are found above an early 18th-century plantation-made sideboard (above). **I**ron gates from a family home in York, S.C., open onto the brick pathways of the color-filled garden and the circular terrace (right).

**T**HE FREDERICK FRASER HOUSE IS AN elegant brick and stucco townhouse constructed by a descendant of John Fraser, one of the Lowcountry's earliest settlers. Fraser, a stout Scotsman, ventured into the Carolina territory around 1700, settling at Pocotaligo near the Coosawhatchee River, not too far from the tribal council assembly of the Yemassee Indians. Fortunately, the Fraser family survived the bloody Yemassee uprising of 1715. By 1800, Frederick Grimke Fraser, John's grandson, was ready to begin construction on his Beaufort townhouse.

One of Beaufort's most graceful houses, the Frederick Fraser house is solidly constructed with 18-inch-thick brick walls. Typical of the period, the exterior was covered with stucco and scored to resemble stone.

Atypical of the period, Fraser selected slender hexagonal columns to support his double porches, a contrast to the more conservative classical columns on other Beaufort houses of the time. Additionally, the Fraser house retains its original entrance stairs.

While Fraser's home has weathered the years well — almost all of the woodwork is original — a 1990s renovation added a glass-enclosed solarium that allows guests the opportunity to enjoy the never-ending color in the adjoining garden.

# The William Wigg Barnwell House

*Portraits of Confederate ancestors stand guard in the boy's room (above). The library contains an extensive collection of volumes on Southern history and literature (right).*

On a balmy September day in 1973, Beaufortonians lined the city streets, holding their breath as moving crews lifted the old Barnwell house off its original foundation on Prince Street and eased the dwelling onto its new site four blocks to the east. Slated for demolition, the house was saved through the intervention of the Historic Beaufort Foundation and Savannah antiques dealer Jim Williams, who purchased, moved, and restored the three-story, Federal-style dwelling.

The townhouse was built in 1816 by the Gibbes brothers as a dowry for their sister, Sarah Reeve Gibbes. Sarah was nicknamed "Sally-Sixteen" for the number of children she bore her husband, William Wigg Barnwell.

The townhouse contained 10 rooms, including a 43-foot reception room. It is doubtful that this room was the setting for social events. A nephew once remarked that William Barnwell "would certainly never have been called an amiable man. ... His temper was severe and his will strong."

Although their son Bower Williamson Barnwell was able to acquire the house after the war, this line of the family did not remain in Beaufort. Subsequently, the elegant home became a boarding house, school, and apartment building. Surprisingly, the house retained much of its original paneling and magnificent stair hall when Williams undertook the meticulous two-year restoration. Due to Williams' exacting nature, the house appears at home in its new surroundings.

# The Miles Brewton Sams House

**A** *collection of antique snuffboxes and portrait miniatures are found among the book-lined shelves of the library* (above).
**M**id-19th-century, tortoise-shell tea caddies and snuffboxes are artfully arranged atop an antique chest (right).
**T**he bust of Napoleon gazes across an 18th-century Rhode Island blanket chest (following spread).

**M**ILES BREWTON SAMS WOULD NOT HAVE recognized his late 1700s home in the early days of the 20th century. Caught up in the late Victorian frenzy to over-embellish, subsequent owners disguised the simple lines of the Sams house with a dizzying array of decorative millwork.

A discriminating collector recognized that an elegant house lay beneath the dressed-up façade. With a discerning eye, he began a thorough restoration in the 1980s. The result is a perfect example of a Beaufort T-shaped house, an appropriate setting for an exceptional collection of American furniture and decorative art.

The collection of outbuildings, including an orchid house, potting shed, and guest house, re-create an assembly of dependencies that might have originally completed the urban landscape.

In the living room, the collection of 18th-century American pieces includes antique mirrors,
Windsor chairs, and a Rhode Island curly maple tea table (left).
Relocated from a nearby neighborhood, the former slave cabin, furnished with
18th- and 19th-century Southern pieces, serves as a guesthouse (above, left).
Lit by a whimsically hung chandelier, the brick patio at the rear of the house
provides wonderful spectator seating for frequent croquet matches
on the expansive lawn (above, right).

## Baptist Church of Beaufort

**B**Y THE 1830S, GREEK REVIVAL STYLE HAD TAKEN A FIRM ARCHITECTURAL HOLD ON SOUTH CAROLINA. IN BEAUFORT, THE STYLE first appeared in residential renovations. Fashion-conscious Beaufortonians dressed up their old-fashioned Federal-style homes in Grecian garb. They abandoned Tuscan columns and delicate porticos for massive full-height galleries incorporating Doric, Ionic, and Corinthian orders. The Baptist Church of Beaufort *(above, left)* was the town's first religious building in the Greek fashion.

The massive brick structure, which cost the congregation $10,000, stood as a testament to the growth of a church that was established in 1804 and had become an influential religious force in the region within a short time.

The first service in the new building was held on April 14, 1844. The temple-front church with two in-antis Doric columns has a perfectly proportioned interior, a three-sided gallery supported by fluted Doric columns, and a coved ceiling embellished with unusually fine plaster ornamentation.

In 1857, the congregation numbered 180 whites and 3,557 slaves, many of whom were served by missions on the islands. During the occupation by Federal troops, the church was used as a hospital for African-American soldiers who inscribed their names on the belfry beams. The current steeple was added in 1961. In 1997, the congregation began an 18-month restoration, ensuring the preservation of one of Beaufort's finest Greek Revival landmarks.

# Tabernacle Baptist Church

**T**HE VICTORIAN GOTHIC ARCHITECTURE OF TABERNACLE BAPTIST CHURCH *(above, middle)* PROVIDES FEW CLUES TO the early history of the building and its site. The earliest surrounding graves date to 1817, perhaps accompanying a praise house erected as early as 1811. In 1834, the Rev. Thomas Fuller, pastor of the Baptist Church of Beaufort, noted that each Wednesday evening he conducted lectures at the "Tabernacle" or black meeting hall on Craven Street. In the 1840s, Fuller held regular services at the Tabernacle while his congregation awaited completion of its nearby Greek Revival building.

After Federal troops entered Beaufort in 1861, Tabernacle Baptist Church became the center for African-American religion. Organized September 1, 1863, by the Rev. Soloman Peck of Boston, Massachusetts, the 500 member congregation formally purchased the building from the Baptist Church of Beaufort in 1867.

A bell tower, the structure's focal point, was added in 1873 and was renovated following the hurricane of 1893. Architectural icing includes pointed, arched stained-glass windows and highly decorative buttresses complete with finials mimicking the roof of the soaring bell tower.

Tabernacle Baptist Church is the final resting place for Robert Smalls, Beaufort's most prominent African-American political figure. The stained-glass windows *(above, right)* are the 20th-century creation of church member Lee Meyers.

# St. Helena's Episcopal Church

THE SPIRE OF ST. HELENA'S EPISCOPAL CHURCH RISES MAJESTICALLY ABOVE THE TOWN'S CANOPIES OF LIVE OAKS. Although the parish was established in 1712, the first church to house St. Helena's congregation was not built until 1724.

In 1769, the congregation replaced the original building, and in 1817, they expanded the facility to the west with the construction of the present tower base with its rusticated corners, pediment, pilasters, fanlight, and tripartite stair window. The church proved too small for the growing congregation. During a major rebuilding program in 1842, much of the church was demolished to ground level. The present side walls were constructed, and the foundations of the 1769 church were used to support the interior galleries. After the renovations were completed, one observer noted, "The Bishop remarked that the church was so enlarged and altered as to be called new."

During the Civil War, Federal troops used St. Helena's as a hospital, uprooting slabs from the churchyard for use as operating tables. In 1866, sailors from the U.S.S. New Hampshire built and donated the current altar.

The chancel was rebuilt after the 1893 hurricane, and a new steeple was added in 1942 according to designs provided by Albert Simons of Charleston. In 1999, the congregation embarked on an ambitious restoration of the building, ensuring the preservation of a house of worship for Beaufort's oldest religious congregation.

# Brick Church at Penn Center

**B**RICK CHURCH IS ONE OF 20 BUILDINGS THAT COMPRISE THE PENN CENTER HISTORIC DISTRICT. THE CHURCH, THE DISTRICT'S oldest building, was built by slaves in 1855 as a place of worship for the Baptist plantation owners on St. Helena Island. The beauty of the structure is its simplicity. The restraint is carried into an austere interior, with simple boxed pews and a three-sided gallery.

With the flight of white plantation owners following the battle of Port Royal Island in 1861, African-Americans took possession of the church, using it as a place of worship and later as a school room and a meeting hall for Penn School.

Penn School, the first educational facility for freedmen in America, was founded in 1862 by Northern abolitionist missionaries. In 1884, the surviving white members of the congregation conveyed the property to the Baptist Church of Beaufort, who leased Brick Church to its black congregation. The surrounding Penn School had grown to include an impressive assemblage of teachers' cottages, dormitories, classrooms, and shop buildings. In the 1950s, Penn School expanded its mission to include a variety of community outreach and lifelong learning services. It continues to serve St. Helena Island and the surrounding community as an educational and conference center. In July 1973, the Baptist Church of Beaufort formally deeded Brick Church to the Brick Baptist Church of St. Helena. In 1974, the National Park Service named Penn Center a National Historic Landmark.

# The Dr. Joseph Johnson House / The Castle

*Family portraits and comfortable furnishings create an intimate feel despite the grand scale of the living room* (above).
*The double staircase is the focal point of the expansive central hall* (right).
*The soft brick walls are covered with a thin layer of plaster. The color is muted and changeable, in shades of gray, tan, and pink* (following spread).

RESTING ON A FULL CITY BLOCK AND SET in the midst of a two-acre garden brimming with azaleas and camellias, The Castle was the last great mansion built in Beaufort before the Civil War.

In 1859, local builder J.S. Cooper constructed a townhouse for Dr. Joseph Johnson. The design drew on Classical and Romantic architectural themes. The six massive octagonal columns are more reminiscent of the tombs of ancient Egypt than the classic temples of imperial Rome. The highly decorated parapet with its stucco Gothic arches rises five feet above the roofline, with four triple chimneys towering above it.

Yet for all its Old World pretensions, The Castle incorporates the familiar T-shaped plan common to most Beaufort houses — the rear rooms extending past the width of the front façade in an attempt to capture the southern breeze.

Like most Beaufort houses, The Castle was confiscated by the Federal government and was used as a Union hospital. Johnson was able to reacquire his home with payment of $2,000 in taxes — a sizable sum made possible by his thriving patent medicine business.

# East Street Victorian

*The shade garden was inspired by old Beaufort gardens and an 1870 guide to suburban home landscaping* (above). *The American Empire table is set with early Flow Blue china over which hangs a Victorian chandelier* (right).

THIS CHARMING VICTORIAN REFLECTS THE fanciful and exuberant architectural ornamentation that was popular in America in the late 19th century. In 1886, in the wake of an economic boom brought on by phosphate mining, German immigrant merchant E.A. Scheper built this dwelling as well as a number of houses on adjoining lots on Craven Street. Scheper may have found inspiration for these houses in a popular pattern book of the era, *Supplement to Bicknell's Village Builder.*

The mass production of architectural millwork and an extended rail system throughout the country made Victorian ornamentation accessible to the most modest home owner. In the late 19th century, variations of Queen Anne and Stick-style architecture began to appear on Beaufort's streets. In a desire to keep up with current fashion, the owners of the city's antebellum mansions began to adorn their classically inspired dwellings with touches of gingerbread.

Restored in 1989–1990, this house retains elements of its original millwork, heart-pine floors, and coal-burning fireplaces. The furnishings reflect a collector's love of 19th-century American decorative arts: the American Empire dining table is set with early Flow Blue china; an ornate Victorian candle and kerosene chandelier lights the table; the ceiling frieze repeats a design by English artist and designer William Morris.

# The Benjamin Chaplin House

**B**ENJAMIN CHAPLIN HAD THIS TOWNHOUSE BUILT IN 1791. THE CONSTRUCTION DATE AND A SET OF initials, perhaps belonging to the carpenter, were uncovered on the stairwell during a 1990s restoration. This unknown carpenter constructed a modest spraddle-roofed cottage, an easily recognizable architectural form prevalent throughout South Carolina.

Chaplin's house is a rare example of an 18th-century plantation house constructed in an urban setting. The broken side-gable or spraddle roof stretches out over the full-width recessed porch. The small cottage originally consisted of two adjoining rooms on the first floor and a half-story above. The interior wallboards retain their original planing marks.

Unlike many of the area planters who chose not to return to Beaufort after the Civil War, the Chaplin family reclaimed a small plantation near Shell Point. Unfortunately, they were unable to recover their modest townhouse. John Judge, a volunteer in one of South Carolina's African-American regiments, purchased the cottage for $640 in the Direct Tax Sale of 1864.

The collection of sewing-related antiques in the sewing room *(above)* includes an 1879 sleeve form, an 1883 sewing machine, and late-19th-century and early-20th-century merchant's cabinets.

# The Esther Foy Jenkins House

From 1908 until 1940, Sears Roebuck and Company provided approximately 450 ready-to-assemble designs for American home builders. Ordered by mail and shipped by rail, the popular houses met the need for well-constructed, inexpensive modern homes. This 1928 bungalow is believed to be a Sears Roebuck Catalog house along with at least three neighboring houses that are nearly identical in design.

   Retaining all of its original woodwork, the Jenkins House is in pristine condition, due in large part to a sensitive homeowner. Encircled by a white picket fence and resting amidst lush paintings, the small bungalow houses a fine collection of English, Italian and American decorative art, including a Waterford chandelier, Chippendale chairs, and Sheffield silver. The shadow box contains 19$^{th}$ and 20$^{th}$ century button hooks.

# The Hepworth-Pringle House

*The Hepworth-Pringle House is considered to be the earliest house in Beaufort (above). Restored to a single-family residence in the 1950s, the house retains the handsome corner cupboard, one of the last remaining pieces of 18th-century cabinetry in Beaufort (right).*

BEAUFORT'S EARLY COLONISTS CAME FROM a pre-industrial England where domestic buildings were built according to medieval traditions. Colonists used traditional frame construction in which large timbers were fitted together with mortise-and-tenon joints and held together with wooden pegs. South Carolina builders copied prevailing fashion by laying brick walls in a Flemish bond and erecting massive T-shaped chimneys, techniques transported to England from the European Low Countries.

In 1717, the Lords Proprietors granted Thomas Hepworth, a prominent Charleston lawyer and later Chief Justice of South Carolina, a lot on the southwest corner of New and Port Royal (Port Republic) streets. The Hepworth house is an excellent example of the type constructed in early 18th-century Carolina. The Dutch influence was obviously apparent to the residents of Beaufort. In 1871, in describing the effects of the Revolution on Beaufort, Dr. John Johnson wrote, "The only remaining memorials of that war within our present view are the two redoubts in the north western suburbs and the little Dutch House on the corner of Port Republic and New Streets."

Before restoration by the Pringle family, the Hepworth house served as a private boys school, a meeting place for local Masons, and as a post-World War II apartment house.

# The Henry McKee House / Robert Smalls House

Enclosed by a moss-covered, open-weave brick fence, the house built for Henry McKee in 1834 contains Federal detailing similar to houses constructed in Beaufort decades earlier. The parlor overmantel with quadrant sunbursts that frame an ellipse is reminiscent of similar woodwork found in John Mark Verdier's 1805 Federal house on Bay Street. The use of a common floor plan and similar interior-decorative motifs reflects the conservative nature of the town's population and perhaps the talents of a single master craftsman who was repeatedly called upon to construct the planters' townhouses.

McKee's house is best known as the home of Robert Smalls, who was born a slave in a cabin at the rear of the property. In 1862, Smalls commandeered a side-wheeler, The Planter, and transported his family and 12 others through Union lines to freedom. With his reward money, Smalls purchased his former master's home. He became one of South Carolina's most prominent African-Americans, serving in the State Senate and House of Representatives, U.S. Congress, and as Customs Collector of the Port of Beaufort. In recognition of his remarkable life and career, Congress designated the house a National Historic Landmark in 1975.

# The Samuel J. Bampfield House

AFTER HIS PURCHASE OF THE HENRY McKEE RESIDENCE ON PRINCE STREET, FORMER SLAVE, congressman, and port collector Robert Smalls acquired most of the surrounding city block, building or moving houses onto the property as homes for his children.

This two-story frame dwelling was home to Smalls' eldest daughter and her husband, Samuel J. Bampfield. An influential public figure in Beaufort, Bampfield served as a state representative, county clerk, and postmaster.

The modestly scaled house was constructed in the 1830s. It has a central hall with rooms on either side and a rear wing that was added later. The double verandas have been replaced by a simple, gable-roofed entrance porch. During a renovation in the 1990s, painters utilized a trompe l'oeil technique, creating the illusion of marble on the simple wooden walls.

# The Secession House

*Mid-19th-century graffiti left by Union soldiers is found in the basement arcade* (above). *Jib doors open onto a first-floor porch with antique wicker furniture. The gateleg dining-room table was made in the 1930s by an owner's grandfather* (right).

EDMUND RHETT, A LEADING SOUTH Carolina secessionist, remodeled an early 19th-century tabby house in the 1840s to create this Greek Revival showplace. Rhett added the necessary double porches, utilizing fluted Ionic columns at the lower level and columns with delicately made Tower of the Winds capitals on the second floor. He also placed elaborate cast-iron balustrades along the arched brick foundation.

Similar to other Beaufort houses positioned close to the street, a delicate curving marble staircase at the eastern corner of the façade provides access to the first-floor porch. Rhett embellished all 10 principal rooms of the house with elaborate Greek Revival cornices and ceiling medallions emblazoned with delicate acanthus leaves.

Rhett was the longtime intendant or mayor of the town, and his fellow Beaufortonians held so much confidence in his leadership that they thought his presence alone would stave off a Yankee invasion.

In November 1861, Port Royal Island fell to Union forces and Rhett's home was confiscated and used for officers' quarters, a hospital, and the Paymaster's office.

Although the once-powerful Rhett died in 1863 while still a refugee, his former residence still bears the name Secession House.

# Okatee River Cottage

In the tapestry of creeks, rivers, marshes, and hummocks in the Lowcountry, river cottages hold a special spot in the architectural landscape. Simplicity and practicality are two hallmarks of river-cottage architecture. Indeed, these two principles stand as reminders of the Lowcountry before its late 20th-century discovery and the rapid development that threatens the simple beauty of the land and waterways.

   This Okatee river cottage exemplifies these simple houses that lend themselves to a lifestyle dictated by the changing tide. Pecky-cypress paneling and the stone fireplace create a warm interior for the living room in this family retreat. A prevalent feature of the river cottage is an ample screened porch that serves as a living room in the warm months. This particular porch has a commanding view of the Okatee River, one of Beaufort County's most pristine estuaries.

# The Edward Means House

**A**FTER THE INVASION OF PORT ROYAL ISLAND BY UNION FORCES IN 1861, NEWSPAPER REPORTERS and war correspondents began sending descriptions of Beaufort and the surrounding Sea Islands to their Northern editors. A special war correspondent sent the following dispatch to the *New York Daily Tribune* in December 1861: "The splendor of the houses and furniture and the beauty of the place may have been exaggerated, but the house of Colonel Edward Means would be called handsome in any town in the North."

The Means house was relatively new when Union forces entered Beaufort, having been completed in early January 1857. Similar in plan to two other houses in Beaufort, the two-story dwelling has a series of spacious reception rooms opening onto south-facing double porches. Shaded by a semicircular porch supported by Ionic columns, the main entrance is on the eastern elevation, providing access to a wide rear hall and an exquisite floating spiral staircase.

Dotted with moss-draped live oaks, the grounds surrounding the noble dwelling are enclosed by an open-weave brick fence covered with delicate Resurrection fern.

# The Thomas Fuller House / Tabby Manse

THOMAS FULLER BUILT HIS HOME ON THE bluff overlooking the river in 1786. It is a two-story, hip-roofed structure with a double-tiered portico supported with slender Tuscan columns. The central hall widens at the rear to accommodate the staircase where a single flight of stairs rises to a landing, divides into two flights, and returns to the second story against the opposite walls of the hall.

The house was constructed of tabby, an early form of concrete made from oyster shells and lime, and the exterior was covered with stucco and scored to resemble stone.

The eight perfectly proportioned rooms, including three completely paneled in heart pine and cypress, have excellent Adam-style mantels with applied cast-plaster panels. Fuller utilized the T-shaped plan, which provided additional cross-ventilation for the rear rooms.

*The pine and cypress paneling and the Adam mantel provide a striking contrast to the modern artwork and contemporary furnishings (above). A Venetian window lights the stairwell and the paintings by Beaufort artist Christian Trask (right).*

Thomas and Elizabeth Fuller reared 12 children in the home, one of whom was Dr. Richard Fuller, a nationally renowned Baptist minister instrumental in the founding of the Southern Baptist Convention. The house was purchased at the Direct Tax Sale of 1864 by Mansfield French, a Methodist minister sponsored by the American Missionary Association. From the 1870s, the home was operated as a guesthouse. The Fuller house became a private residence in 1969 and was christened "Tabby Manse."

# The Henry Farmer House

**I**n the foreground, clerodendrum and
odontonema add splashes of color to the
entrance of the house (above).
**F**ormal parterres contain an amazing variety of
Southern plant material (right).

**T**HE HENRY FARMER HOUSE IS NOTE-
worthy for its Federal architecture as well as
for its historic gardens. Constructed in 1810,
the dwelling incorporates all of the elements
one would expect to find in an elegant
Federal-style home. The double-tiered portico
with its denticulated pediment is supported
by Tuscan columns. Delicate fanlights rest in
finely articulated door surrounds, and spacious
hallways provide easy access to a series of
well-proportioned and expertly appointed
rooms. From these interior spaces and the
front portico, visitors have the opportunity
to gaze upon Beaufort's oldest gardens.

While honeymooning in Italy in the 1830s,
Richard and Charlotte Fuller, the home's
second owners, collected the first of many
specimen plants for their garden, most
notably the Roman laurel and Guernsey lily. In the late 20th century, the Fuller's ancient garden
fell into the care of Southern garden authority Frances Parker, who added parterres to the side
garden to extend the formal framework.

Edged with boxwood, mondo grass, and clipped serissa, the parterres contain a profusion
of plant material that provides a continuous stream of seasonal color. The Fullers' brick wall and
Roman laurel hedge remain as key elements of the overall garden design.

**T**he living room showcases Spanish-made and Jacobean furniture and a painting
by Beaufort artist Marguerite Grossenbach Barnum (left).
**A**n antique ormolu chandelier hangs above the Spanish-made, Louis XVI-style table.
The portrait is by Richard Lofton, c. 1930 (above).

# The James Rhett House

**N**ot built until c. 1886, the house quickly assumed the air of an antebellum house, fitting in quite well with its older neighbors (above). **R**hett embellished his home with elaborate plaster moldings, ceiling medallions, and slate mantels in the late Renaissance Revival style (right).

**T**HE ARCHITECTURAL DESIGN OF THE JAMES Rhett House is similar to scores of other Beaufort dwellings that were constructed to take advantage of the prevailing southern breeze.

With wide double verandas embracing two sides, the house originally was one room deep, allowing maximum cross-ventilation even in the stifling summer months.

Here, however, one sees a familiar Beaufort-style home dressed up in late 19th-century Victorian attire with double-height bay windows and Eastlake-style moldings.

While one would expect the verandas to be adorned with turned posts and Victorian gingerbread commonly found on late 19th-century porches, Rhett selected traditional classical columns.

During an extensive 1999 renovation, the original portion of the house was restored and a seamless rear addition was added.

# Dean Hall

*T*he plantation home is pleasantly situated on
the banks of Huspah Creek (above).
**A**n 18th-century Charleston clock by
William Lee (1768–1803) rests on the
South Carolina-quarried slate mantel in the
living room. A rare Confederate
officer's sword and scabbard are displayed
on the North Carolina sideboard, c. 1800,
above which hangs The Courier,
a painting by N.C. Wyeth (right).

IN THE 18TH CENTURY, CAROLINA GOLD,
a variety of rice, transformed the young South
Carolina colony into a wealthy agrarian society.
Dean Hall represents the rise of the great
Lowcountry plantation during this time.

Before Dean Hall was moved to its
current site on Huspah Creek, it stood on a
peninsula in the Cooper River in Berkeley
County, a 3,200-acre rice plantation settled
in 1725 by a baronet, Alexander Nesbett
of Dean, Scotland.

In 1827, William Augustus Carson
acquired the plantation and implemented
a complex "tidal" system of rice cultivation,
a profitable method that required attentive
management. Carson replaced the Nesbett
house with one suited to year-round
habitation. While some architectural historians
believe that the form of Dean Hall and
similar plantation houses originated in the
West Indies, others argue that it developed
independently in South Carolina in response
to a similar climate.

Supported by tapered columns and reached by a double flight of stairs, the encircling piazza
ensures shade all day. Resting on a basement-level arcade, the raised upper floors are perfectly

*The corner cupboard showcases a collection of baskets by Tennessee basket maker Mary Prator. The dry-brush watercolor,* U.S. Navy, *is by Andrew Wyeth, and the small painting of roses is by Jamie Wyeth (previous spread).*
*The dining room features an American Federal inlaid dining table from Virginia, c. 1820, and a birch and tulip poplar hunt board that was made in Athens, Georgia, c. 1810 (left).*
*Jamie Wyeth's* Vidalia Onions *and a Georgia-made, black-walnut lazy-Susan table are found in the kitchen (above, left).*
*A rare South Carolina "bamboo" Chippendale chair can be found in the bathroom (above, right).*

positioned to catch even the slightest breeze, while the broad central hallway allows cool air to pass through lofty rooms. The brick walls help keep the interior cooler in summer and warmer in winter.

In 1909, the Carson family sold Dean Hall to Benjamin Kittredge of New York who transformed his hunting preserve into Charleston's Cypress Gardens.

After his death, the house and surrounding acreage were sold as an industrial site.

Slated for demolition in 1971, the house was moved to its present site on Huspah Creek north of Beaufort.

Beautifully restored, Dean Hall is home to an exceptional collection of American fine and decorative art.

# The George Parsons Elliot House

*The interior is a successful space with gilded cornices and moldings and elaborate plasterwork (above and right).*

THE GEORGE PARSONS ELLIOT HOUSE marks the beginning of the great parade of Beaufort mansions found along the western end of Bay Street.

An imposing residence for one of Beaufort's most prominent and well-connected families, the Elliot house is a naïve expression of the Greek Revival style. The massive, awkwardly spaced Doric columns are oddly juxtaposed with a very late Federal-style fanlight. Constructed in an era when porches were essential outdoor living spaces, the Elliot house oddly had no upper veranda.

Elliot copied the floor plan of his brother's house, the Anchorage, located on the next block. These two houses are variations of the T-shaped Beaufort plan. Here, the rear rooms extend past the width of the façade as full-height bay windows.

Shortly before the Civil War, Elliot sold his home to Dr. William Jenkins, one of the richest men in Beaufort. Confiscated and converted to a hospital during the Federal occupation, the home later sold in a tax auction to George Holmes, a native of Bedford, N.Y., who served as Intendant (Mayor) of Beaufort during Reconstruction.

Holmes redecorated several rooms with fashionable Aesthetic-movement furniture, mantels, pier mirrors, and window treatments, all of which survive and are in the collection of the Historic Beaufort Foundation.

# Laurens Street Cottage

*The living room is the setting for
an extensive collection of antiques,
including the c. 1815 convex mirror
with Sandwich glass girandoles (above).
Although expanded, the home has
retained its simple lines and
pleasing façade (right).*

**B**EAUFORT IS FILLED WITH SMALL GRACEFUL townhouses of pleasing proportions. Contructed around 1840, this diminutive vernacular cottage consisted of three rooms and a side porch. The side porch was later enclosed, and a new porch facing Laurens Street was added to the home.

Exotic 18th-century Chelsea porcelain birds and a c. 1759 Sevres bowl signed by Jacques Buteux adorn the mantel in the living room. The Boston andirons and the Hepplewhite serpentine-front card table are late 18th century.

A collection of fine Chinese ivory, export china, and an early 19th-century bronze Buddha from Thailand complement the American and English pieces.

# The John Joyner Smith House

**E**ight massive Doric columns
rise to support a cornice rich with Greek
Revival detailing (above).
**J**ib windows provide access to the porch and a
sweeping view of Beaufort's bay (right).
**T**he double parlors boast some
of Beaufort's finest and most intricate
plasterwork (following spread).

**T**HE WIDE DOUBLE PIAZZAS OF THE JOHN
Joyner Smith house offer an unparalleled view
of the Beaufort River and the Intracoastal
Waterway. The home also provides one of
Beaufort's most unusual architectural curiosities
— an elaborate false front door set in an
exceptionally detailed Adam-style surround.

One of three Beaufort houses with similar
floor plans, the John Joyner Smith house has
connecting double parlors, a rear stairhall,
and a side entrance reached by a flight of
white marble steps. With no central hall, the
elaborate false entrance is an obvious conces-
sion to symmetry. The false door is flanked by
tripartite jib windows that allow easy access
from the parlors to the columned galleries.

Brig. Gen. Isaac Ingalls Stevens selected the
Smith's house as his headquarters following
the fall of Port Royal Island to the Union in
1861. Stevens' respect for private property
and his responsible stewardship of the home

may account for the retention of many of the dwelling's original features.

Following the war, the house changed hands several times before its purchase in 1910 by
C.E. McLeod, Sr., the grandfather of the present owner and the first of four generations of the
family to enjoy the history and beauty of the elegant home.

# The Thomas Hazel House

*An American walnut plantation desk c. 1830 flanks the French doors leading to the sunroom. A painting of a Charleston church by Guy Lipscomb, a Columbia artist, hangs over the mantel (above).*
*The house retains an extraordinary amount of original glazing in the windows, transoms, and sidelights (right).*

THE FIRST GREAT WAVE OF HOME construction in Beaufort followed the Revolutionary War, lasting through the early years of the 19th century. In the 1850s, fueled by a growing cotton-based economy, a second building boom began, and the eastern section of town, near Black's Point, hummed with the sounds of new construction. House builders incorporated the best architectural devices found in older Beaufort homes, particularly the double-tiered gallery.

In 1852, Thomas Hazel completed a two-and-a-half-story dwelling for his bride on land given to him by Joseph Hazel, his father. He finished his verandas with a balustraded parapet, which today is one of the last remaining examples of what was once a common feature of Beaufort houses. He embellished the interior with Greek Revival black and white marble mantels and dentil moldings.

Purchased successively by three grooms as wedding gifts for their wives, the house is known locally as the honeymoon cottage.

# White Hall Plantation

*Engine designer Charles Lawrance remodeled the White Hall plantation house in the Colonial Revival style (above). The magnificent stable was designed by Charleston architectural firm Schmitt Sampson Walker (right).*

Toward the end of the 19th century, South Carolina's mild climate and abundant game attracted the attention of wealthy Northern industrialists searching for winter hunting retreats.

Old South Carolina plantations were now owned by America's leaders in finance, transportation, and industry — Vanderbilt, Hutton, Havemeyer, Luce, and duPont. Some of these men erected Colonial Revival houses, typically five-part plan dwellings faithful in spirit to 18th-century Tidewater and Lowcountry models.

In 1927, Charles Lawrance, an aircraft engine designer who contributed to Lindbergh's Spirit of St. Louis, acquired White Hall, Nathaniel Heyward's former plantation. Heyward's descendants constructed a simple two-story house in 1890 to replace the original family residence that was burned by Sherman's troops in 1865. Lawrance added the full-height portico, hyphens, and flanking rooms, creating one of the region's best Colonial Revival-style homes. Later, he enclosed the east veranda and re-created a number of outbuildings using early maps to position structures on original sites.

Subsequent owners continued Lawrance's tradition of adding appropriate outbuildings and support structures. A large stable is the most recent addition to the ensemble.

# The Lewis Reeve Sams House

*Sams selected both Doric and Ionic columns as supports for his double verandas (above). The mural in the entrance hall created by Robert Gleason depicts Beaufortonians watching the ships come into Port Royal harbor in the 19th century (right).*

IN THE BEGINNING OF THE 20TH CENTURY, three antebellum mansions lined lower Bay Street, offering an impressive welcome to visitors arriving by boat at the end of Carteret Street. The Fullers and the Elliotts, two of Beaufort's most prominent families, secured choice waterfront lots and erected late 18th-century Federal-style dwellings. In 1852, Lewis Reeve Sams, a wealthy planter who owned half of Datha (Dataw) Island, joined his neighbors and began construction of a Greek Revival mansion that dominated the end of the street.

Sams employed heavy door surrounds with transoms and sidelights, dentil work along the cornice, and a paneled parapet. The marble entrance steps were an opulent touch, signaling to visitors the owner's wealth and the rich interior that awaited them, which included marble mantels and decorative plaster moldings. In 1869, the Sams' family sold their residence to George Waterhouse, a native of Lyman, Maine, who became a prominent business and civic leader.

In late January 1907, a great fire swept the waterfront and turned northeast, reaching as far as Hancock Street on Black's Point. The fire destroyed blocks of businesses, municipal buildings, and residences, including two of the mansions on lower Bay Street. Waterhouse's mansion, however, was saved by the frantic efforts of his cotton gin workers.

# The Elizabeth Barnwell Gough House

**A** *Palladian window illuminates the*
*landing of the staircase* (above).
**T***he house is constructed of tabby, covered with*
*stucco, and scored to imitate stone* (right).
**T***he 18th-century furniture in the dining room*
*includes a diminutive Newport serpentine*
*sideboard, a Boston-made Queen Anne*
*drop-leaf table, and a New England*
*Hepplewhite dining table* (following spread).

BEAUFORT PLANTERS HAD MANY SOCIAL
and economic ties to Charleston. By the
1770s, elegant buildings based on European
models were being erected on almost every
street in Charleston. It is not surprising that
wealthy Beaufortonians, including Elizabeth
Barnwell Gough, looked to Charleston for
architectural inspiration and that a small
group of Beaufort buildings was obviously
modeled after the Miles Brewton House,
c. 1765, one of the finest expressions of
English Palladian architecture in America.

A granddaughter of "Tuscarora Jack
Barnwell," a local Indian fighter, Elizabeth
Barnwell defied her parents in 1772 and
married Richard Gough of James Island.

Described as rebellious, hot-tempered,
and independent, Elizabeth left her husband
within the year and returned with her
daughter to Beaufort.

With money provided for her benefit at
her father's death in 1775, Elizabeth Gough
began construction of one of Beaufort's most elegant Federal-style dwellings.

Delicate Tuscan columns support the Palladian-inspired double-tiered portico, whereas the
interior illustrates aspects of the emerging Adams and Federal styles. Unfortunately, the name of

the master builder who executed the intricately carved cypress paneling and cornices in the two drawing rooms and second-floor ballroom is unknown. Elizabeth Gough may have engaged a trained master builder from Charleston or perhaps a local craftsman armed with a series of recently arrived English pattern books. Whoever the artisan, the resulting interiors were the most fashionable in the small river port town of Beaufort in the late 18th century.

In the early 19th century, the elegant Palladian mansion was the boyhood home of Robert Barnwell Rhett, Elizabeth Gough's grandson, a leader in the States' Rights movement and a principal secessionist. During the Civil War, the house was used as a hospital. In the 20th century, it became a kindergarten before being divided into apartments.

After a lengthy restoration in 1976, the house once again became a single-family residence. That year, with the assistance of the Historic Beaufort Foundation, the delicate cypress paneling that was removed from the southeast parlor in the 1920s was returned. With the assistance of nationally recognized experts, a more extensive restoration of the home was undertaken in 1996.

*The kitchen reflects the owners' appreciation of local folk art. A collection of 19th-century doorstops graces the mantel. Flanking the window, the large painting on tin by the late Sam Doyle of St. Helena Island is of Dr. Buzz, a traditional Lowcountry voodoo practitioner* (left).
*The house is largely furnished in exceptional 18th-century pieces, including a Massachusetts Hepplewhite mahogany wing chair, a Philadelphia Chippendale tea table, and a walnut and gilt Chippendale looking glass* (above).
*The paneled ballroom is one of Beaufort's most beautiful interior spaces* (following spread).